Gimme 5:
15 Things You Should Know to Start and Sustain a Business Beyond 5 Years

By
Dr. Zeboye A. Doctor

Dr. Doctor Teach Me How to Fish Foundation
Jacksonville, FL

Printed in the United States of America

ISBN: 9781688442375

Contact:
Dr. Zeboye A. Doctor
Dr. Doctor Teach Me How to Fish Foundation
drdrteachmehowtofish@gmail.com
Jacksonville, FL

Dedication

This book is dedicated to my ancestors that persevered in uncertain times in order that I may exist today.

To my wife, Dr. Nekeshia Doctor, for her quiet spirit that says push yourself like I know you can and be the best you that your creator has made you to be.

To my children, who I am giving my life to ensure that they have the experiences that I did not.

To my grandmother whose love, worth ethic, and dedication spoke to me and said "No excuses, work hard, and provide for your family.

To my fraternity brother and friend, Tramene Maye, thank you for your brotherly love and support over the years.

To my family, coaches, spiritual leaders, elders, brothers, sisters, classmates, teammates, co-workers who are too many to name that have imparted precious pearls in my life, I say thank you.

Table of Contents

Acknowledgements

From the deepest core of my innermost being, I exalt the ancestors.

To my ancestors who were oppressed, I thank them for their contributions to this world in the sciences, arts, religions, mathematics, inventions, business, health, finances, and unknown arenas as we know has been hidden, that we are uncovering.

To the spirit of our ancestors that says "Never give up, be determined. Don't be afraid. Trust in yourself above all. Know thyself and know God. Know God and know thyself."

To that same spirit that says, "Don't give up. You are more than you've ever been told and if you seek the truth, at times even in the darkest places, you will find it. To that spirit, I say thank you.

To the spirit of our ancestors that says, "Although you have made it, you MUST, you MUST, you MUST return to help your people that desire the same and yet feel that they do not have that which is necessary to free themselves in abundance. I say thank you.

Biography

Dr. Zeboye A. Doctor

- Graduated from William M. Raines Senior High School in 1998, where he was a member of the National Honor Society and the 1997 4-A State Football team
- Graduated Cum Laude from Alabama Stated in 2002 with a Bachelor of Science degree in Biology
- Graduate of Sherman College of Chiropractic in 2006.
- Graduate of Miles Law School in 2015
- In 2007, founded A-Z Gonstead Chiropractic Clinic in Jacksonville, Florida
- In 2010, founded DR. DOCTOR Disc Injury and Spinal Care Clinic.
- In 2018, established DR. Doctor Teach Me How to Fish Foundation, a 501c3 nonprofit organization for urban youth.
- Lifetime member of Omega Psi Phi Fraternity, Inc.

Chapter 1
It's All in the Name

Main Principle

It is important that one decides HOW they want to be identified in their business.

The name of your business is the "principal force" that drives the vision; sets one apart from others. But, most importantly, it is a statement to yourself, then others of WHO and WHAT you are.

Making a decision of how you want to be identified as CEO of your company is extremely vital. As the CEO, it all begins with YOU. You must have clarity not only about that which you desire to do in business to impact the world, but also the name that you attach to it......

It's not about necessarily about being different. The purpose of writing this book is not to say that I (we) am different. But, to merely put the thoughts that I have had in my mind over the past several years to action, reducing it to words so that someone who is thinking about starting a business; has the opportunity to start a business. It is also for someone that has been in fear of starting of business, but unsure how to start a business. Someone who is tired of "clocking in and out" in someone else's company and they are right there at the edge of the diving board; the edge of the ledge and they are ready to jump. They are definitely not jumping to their death, but ultimately, they are jumping into their life. They are jumping into their being. They are coming into the person, power, creation in which they were created and designed to be. So, it's not about being different, it's just about giving someone the tools to start and sustain their business that they simply may not know are out there.

There are many people who move out of fear. I, myself, at one point in time because I was in the darkness from the false indoctrinations introduced to me as a boy in my younger life, I know how that is. It is important to not allow fear to drive you and your decisions. Don't allow fear to stop you. Don't even use fear as a motivation.

Look at it from a different perspective. Allow your success to drive you. Let your thoughts of being more than what you presently are be your motivating and driving force. So, when you think about the name of your business, it should be whatever YOU think that it should be. Go deep into your innermost self.

> "I am what I am."
>
> "I am what you think I am."
>
> "I am not what you think I am, but I am everything I need to be and that's in my name."
>
> Dr. Zeboye A. Doctor

Listen to yourself. Listen to that power; Listen to that quiet, still voice and see what comes to you as to the name that you should call your vision. In time, that name will take on a form of its own or it will come to itself.

Most importantly, you have to give it time. So, no fear. Think on a name. See what speaks to you. Determine what resonates in your spirit. Then, move on it.

When Do We Begin?

You must act NOW to build and establish the businesses and enterprises that you have been restless about. You cannot wait until you obtain a certain amount of money, specific status quo, level of expertise that you think is necessary before the world is introduced to your business and service. There are individuals, prospects that is, that are waiting on you right now to show up and impact lives through your products and services.

Notes For Me:

1. What type of business do I envision?

2. What is the name of my new business?

3. Who do I serve in my business? Who is my avatar?

Chapter 2:

To Incorporate or Not to Incorporate...That's the Question

Main Principle

Will you take all of the RISK in your own personal name for your business?

In Chapter 1, you had to decide on the name of your business. You also had to make a decision on what you were going to call yourself and hold out to the word. Now that you have decided on your business name, you should feel a sense of relief and joy because now you know what you want others to know you as.

The beautiful thing about starting a business or businesses is that if you don't like that business, you can always start another. So, don't worry about it.

It's just that simple.

You get ideas that come to you all of the time and that next idea could be your next big thing, could be THE NEXT BIG or your very next business. So, once you've decided on the name of business, now you have to make a decision on the type of company you're going to have.

Well, what do I mean by that?

You may decide to be a sole proprietor. A sole proprietor is an individual who starts a business in their name or the name of the business is just that. It's just a name. It's not incorporated. It's tied to that individual's social security number and they do the work in that manner.

The Risk

The drawback to having a business in your name or directly tied to your social security number is like a wild dog on someone's property and children are coming down the street.

If your animal is wild. If your animal is not tamed or obedient and is not aware that it is in a domestic situation, your wild dog can come and attack a child coming down the street. And what happens to that child if that child is attacked by the wild dog?

That child has a parent or guardian that is responsible for them. In addition to the parent or guardian taking the child to get the necessary medical attention for the injuries the child has sustained. That parent may want you, being the owner of the dog, to not only pay for the physical injuries that they child sustained, but the mental injuries that the child sustained, and any other financial hardships that the family has or will incur as a result of her your wild untamed animal being in a domestic environment.

So, you may want to really consider incorporating your business into something such as unlimited liability company; a corporation so that you can do this to your animal. This allows you to put your animal into a fence and protect you and your animal from other forces if something ever happened

You must ask yourself, "*am I going to take all of the risk in my own personal name?*

You may be a person who has had a history of quote on quote, bad credit. Maybe something happened, seen or unforeseen. Maybe you didn't have the guidance of family members to teach you how to manage your money; to teach you how to run a bank account; manage debt or even work with credit.

You may have just come to a point in life where you desire to start over or you're working on your idea and incorporating is the best way to do that. Because once you have started your LLC or start that corporation, now you have in essence given birth to an entity; a being or a quazi person with a name separate from your birth name with a social security number known as tax ID number or employee identification number (EIN) You have given you a new chance at life through the means of a corporation or quazi person, but that corporation is just that, numbers on a piece of paper.

It cannot move.

It cannot breathe.

It cannot see.

And it cannot grow WITHOUT you.

You are the eyes, ears, nose, mouth, hands, lungs, and heartbeat.

You are the lifeline of that corporation.

The reader will decide what's different about this book. The beautiful thing about a book is that you can never judge it by its cover. You must open the book. You must read the book and gather the information necessary from the book to change or transform your life.

The thing about this book that I guarantee is this, if you read this book and apply this book, when you are done, you will undoubtedly have a company or business. You will undoubtedly have a rebirth of life within the palm of your hands. You will undoubtedly have your future. The only question that remains is whether or not you're going to be consistent and persistent. Are you going to put in the hard work, effort, and time necessary to give you that chance and put you where you see yourself in your mind? And that part is solely up to YOU.

This book is application. There is a quote that says, "Faith without works is dead." There is no reason whatsoever that you just read this book for information purposes. If you're not going to put the words that I have reduced to writing while riding down the road into action.

Literally, my head was pounding.

My body was tight.

My stomach was turning.

My mouth was saying SPEAK.

Not Another Minute or Second

The core of my being was saying, "Not another day! You must get this out. You must put this book into action. You are not being the best that you can be because what's in you, you have not told anyone else. And now is that time."

> **"So faith by itself, if it has no works, is dead."**
>
> James 2:17
> (Revised Standard Version)

So, application is the key. Putting it into action is the key. I remember hearing a former spiritual leader vividly say, "the cemetery is full of treasure."

I said to myself, what did he mean by that?"

He said, "there were a lot people that died and they had treasures within them that the world never got a chance to see because that vision; that passion for that new business that you have inside of you right now, until it comes out of you into full manifestation, it is just that. It is a treasure. It is hidden and if you don't move on it, it will be dead, laying in the cemetery in you.

"Put a fence around it and protect it from ALL invaders, foreign and domestic."

Dr. Zeboye A. Doctor

Don't be that person.

Work to get everything in you that you possibly can, out of you.

That's GREATNESS!

That's POWER!

And that's what we are doing with this book.

<u>Notes For Me:</u>

1. Talk to an attorney about incorporating my business.

2. Speak with a Certified Public Accountant (CPA).

3. Contact or visit a small business center for assistance if I cannot handle this process myself.

4. Visit the Secretary of State website to search if the name that you have chosen is available. Also, use the site to formerly file your articles.

Chapter 3:
Dealing with Uncle Sam

Main Principle

Do not take your eyes off of your vision.

By now you know the name of your business. You have decided whether to incorporate or not to incorporate. You may have even decided on whether or not within your corporation if it will be a partnership, limited liability company or an association.

In Chapter 2, you were given the thought of incorporating versus not incorporating or sole proprietorship. Now, in so many regards, it is time to deal with "Uncle Sam." You know what, that old man with that top hat dressed in red, white, and blue with his little goatee pointing at you, me, and all of us for a little bit more of the money that we have in our pockets, company or banks; the assets that we have acquired from working our businesses.

Listen, this is where we have to deal with Uncle Sam.

Which Way Do I Go?

It is imperative that when you start your business that if you are not a sole proprietor and that in having a sole proprietorship, you are already aware that it's being tied to your individual social security number. But, if you have chosen the route to incorporate and begin the process to go to the Internal Revenue Service (IRS) with your corporate name, you must also think and act on whether or not your individual state requires this.

This will require you to contact Secretary of State to find out if it permissible. With the Secretary of State, you will search for and register the name of your company so that you can hold out to the world that you desire to do business in your name in that state. Once you have decided on the name of your business, if it's not your individual name, and you decide you will incorporate, now you are dealing with the Secretary of State for the name of your company.

The name of your company should be distinct and different from all other business names. Every company is different.

Now, it's time to go to the Internal Revenue Service website at www.irs.gov. Once you are on the website, you would click on "Start a New Business." The website is generally user friendly. And this book is merely just that.

As stated before, this book is to be used for informational purposes for that nolvist that desires to start a business. At some point, I strongly recommend that if you want to be successful in business that you seek legal and professional advice from a qualified and reputable attorney to assist you with getting your business going. Most importantly, seek the advice of a Certified Public Accountant (CPA) or a tax attorney so that you can be guided in the proper direction of operating your business and you do not fall victim to some of the pitfalls that are out there due to the lack of knowledge.

But, do not choose your CPA or tax attorney without first conducting some research on your own and interviewing at least three individuals. You must do that.

Let's not lose sight of the fact that you definitely must apply for and receive your tax ID or employer ID number. This process takes as little as five (5) minutes and you can receive that information immediately at www.irs.gov. But, as you may already know, if you have begun to investigate or pressed the button to register the legal name of your company in the state you desire to do business, some states will allow you to receive your corporate documents the same day in minutes.

However, if you're like me and live in the state of Florida, this state has changed their process a tad bit where they will usually have your documents available to you online within fourteen days, which is the new normal post Covid-19.

The beautiful thing about it is, I know that you've had this burning desire inside of you to have your business for some time now. How do I know? Well, I'm glad you asked.

I know this because if you are reading this book, you have had some questions that have not been answered. If you are reading this book, you want to try and pick my brain and find out something that you did not previously know. If you are reading this book, maybe you did not have the right mentor or enough mentors or guidance to where you could have the questions that you wanted answered.

So, you decided to pick up this book after taking a look at the cover and now you are reading this book and we are answering the very same questions that you have had or currently having because we had them as well and went through the challenges. And that is why we can tell you because we've gone through it.

Again, it is important to know that this book is a step-by-step informational guide to get you going. We want to get you moving!

In my professional opinion, these are the basic things that every business owner, potential business owner, striving, aspiring business owner needs to KNOW and DO before they start their business now or soon thereafter.

If you start and formulate bad habits from the beginning; if you get misconceptions from others in the beginning who have not had their own business or run a business, you're taking advice from sources that are not founded and cannot direct you to places to refer to double-check what they are saying to you, then chances are, you are going to fall in a pitfall and get discouraged about being in business and it just may frighten you from business and place you back in that "rat race" of punching a time clock and working to make someone else's vision thrive whether than working on your own. There is nothing wrong with supporting someone else's vision, we need that in society.

Much is Required

As stated in prior chapters, you must be consistent. You must be persistent. You must be willing to put in the hard work, dedication, and sacrifice necessary to put you, your family or future family in the position that you see yourself in your mind. And that process...that thing takes TIME.

> **"Every one to whom much is given, of him will much be required..."**
>
> Luke 12:48
> (Revised Standard Version)

You cannot focus and be concerned about what others have going on.

You must put your head down and focus on the task(s) you have at hand and bring your head up as necessary to get food, water, rest; to de-stress, but do not forget your purpose, your motivation, your goals you have set for yourself. Do not take your eyes off of your *vision*.

Chapter 4:
Uncle Sam's Cousin

Main Principle

Check with your local area government or departments in which you live to determine all that is needed to conduct business in your local area.

Once you deal with the federal government with setting up your Employee Identification Number (EIN) and obtaining your EIN number for your business; deciding if you were going to incorporate or not incorporate; and in most cases, you decided to incorporate; determining your name that you desire to do business in during the beginning stages of starting your new business; and you've reached out to the Internal Revenue Services to obtain your tax ID number, now what you have to think about dealing with is....Uncle Sam's Cousin.

Meet Uncle Sam's Cousin

Uncle Sam's cousin is the local government in which you are situated or will do business. Once you have satisfied what we discussed in the previous chapters, you want to check with the local area government or departments to determine which departments that you may need to visit, specifically in the state of Florida, you would visit the Tax Collector's office. In your local Tax Collector's office and with their division, you would obtain your business license.

The purpose of your business license is to let individuals know in the local or in your municipality or your county that you have started a business in that local or you're acting as a sole proprietor tied to your individual, given social security

---

number, and you're conducting business in that local area. When you deal with Uncle Sam's cousin, he is going to charge you a fee in most cases. And in the country in which we live in known as the United States, all cases of doing business because they say that they receive money and generate funds for taking care of our local areas by charging you a TAX or a fee to conduct business.

So, if you happen to be in the service industry, you may have to obtain a business license that identifies you in the service industry. And if you have a facility in which you are running your business from, you're going to have to pay a fee for that as well. But, it is advised that you seek information from qualified, personnel and check with your local area government to find out specifically what you need for your local.

Again, this book is for informational purposes to help clear up any questions that you may have or to act as a guide to get you on the road to having your own business. So, doing the paperwork necessary to have the business license for your area is something that you must do your due diligence to find out whether it is a requirement or not. It is not hard, it is not easy, it is doable.

Another component you must think about as well, at some point, is the tangible property tax in which we will discuss in the coming chapters. So, Uncle Sam's cousin is known as your "local government." Work to reach out to your local government to find out what things are necessary for you to do in order to do business in that local. And if you do not already know anyone or if you do know someone who is working in the industry that you're in, reach out to them to seek their advice; pick their brain on the things that they did in order to start their business. However, avoid seeking advice from just one source, check with multiple individuals or sources because what was required for one person in the area of business that they are engaged in may or may not be required for you.

But, do not see this as a lot of work. Do not look at this as something that you cannot do. Do not let that thing called *FEAR* rise up from the dead. Keep it buried. As a matter of fact, dig it up, set it on fire to never rise again.

These are simply things that you did not know that now as a result of reading this book, you are coming into the knowledge and the light of and it's up to you to act on it so that you can be what it is that you desire to the fullest. Do not be afraid when you call and say, "I need help or I am just starting my business."

Price to Pay

One thing that I have noticed is that everything has a price tag on it and sometimes if you spend your time reading, reading, reading or paying for this and paying for that, you could have already started your business. But, because you did not begin to act on starting your business, you spent a lot of your money trying to find out about this, that or the other instead of getting started. Some people are in the business of selling books and if you buy too many books or buy everyone's book on every topic that you've ever known or thought about that might interest you, what are you going to have to put into your business. But, maybe buying books from others is the business that you're in.

So, I don't want to offend you, but for that person that does not fit that mold, there is a lot of free information out there. Maybe even visiting your local library or using that tool that you may or may not be reading my book from or listening to me on so called technology and putting that tool to use and browsing the internet to research, whether it be videos or links to find answers to the very questions that you have in your mind. You will be surprised at what you find out if you were to begin to look up those things that you're interested in surrounding your business. If there are five or ten results that you discover that are out there, the only cost that you would have to pay for the results, the resources or links, you researched is *TIME.*

So, take the time to read and from reading those five to ten results you should begin to find out the commonalities within those results. And out of those five to ten resources, you will also discover some differences. But, above all, take the commonalities because at least they all agree on these facts. The things that are different from one individual to another, may be the thing that they may use to separate them from the rest of the pack.

Set Apart

At some point in time, you will discover some things that will separate you from the pack.

That's just what it is. Something that you decided that you had to do or did that separated you from others. And it's not bad and it may not be good, it's just what you did.

As it has been stated numerous times in prior chapters, this book is for informational purposes. But, at the end of the day, if you do not take this information and work to apply it, you could have simply donated monies to my foundation listed on the front inside cover of this book entitled, Dr. Doctor Teach Me How to Fish Foundation." In this organization, you can donate monies to helping the youth in this city, state, country, and world gain exposure on how to be what you are currently reading to become...

a business owner,
a better person,

and productive citizen in this city, state, country, and in this world.

Chapter 5:
Getting to It

Main Principle

It's time to get to work on how you want your business to look.

Aspiring business owners, it's time to get to work on how you want your business to look.

As we've continued to provide this step-by-step guide to educate the reader from beginning to end. Look at this here as a birth process. Before you can give birth to any idea, the seed must be planted. Before that seed is planted, you have to pick the right fertile soil in order to give that seed the nutrients necessary to ensure its survival.

Once that seed is planted in the soil at the right depth, at the right time, there must be water that is given to that seed. There must be enough oxygen given to that seed for that seed to sprout and break through the ground. In order to grow to become what it's designed to become. And right now, it's time for you to break through the ground to become and start to put into action where you see your business and how you see your business. So now it's time to break the physical ground and choose your location.

Everyone has a vision in their head for how they see their business; where they see their business; the people that they desire to serve in their business. The type of money that they desire to generate and allow others to generate in their business. What you see in your head right now or may even have reduced to writing is not any different than anyone else that has a business at its core.

So, do not, as we have said before, let fear stop you. Do not let fear drive you. Do not let fear motivate you. Let success, let the energy, the passion, the feeling that you get when you think about your vision, become a reality, becoming a reality.

Let that be what you use in deciding this location. You also want to make sure that you do this when you decide your location. Think about who ultimately in your mind you're going to serve. Based upon you thinking about who you're going to serve, that's where your location needs to be. People will come along and try to put you in places that do not fit.

Think about this scenario, have you ever tried on a pair of shoes at the department store and you go in there and a salesperson asks you, "what size do you wear?"

You reply, "give me a size 13."

You put the shoes on and it's tight around your toes or between the ball of your feet, where your toes are or right at the arch. Have you ever gotten that feeling?

Or have you ever felt it wasn't enough room in the front of your toes and the salesperson tells you that they could give you get a half size bigger? Or we'll go up another size because the shoes run small? What I have learned is whenever you give someone your shoe size, it's a number and a letter. So, I may wear a size 13 and that may be my length, but my letter is not M for medium, I'm actually a 13 wide, which is a "D" or 4E. That's my comfort level.

So, you must pick the location that is going to best serve your needs. You're going to want to choose your location where the demographics or the people that you desire to serve are going to come. Sometimes the best thing we can do is go directly to the people that we desire to serve, whether than to listen to what someone else says and put us in an entirely different location and we're paying high rent. We have to do an extensive build out. Money that you just may not have.

And if you are like me. You didn't have a fund that someone in your family set aside for you to start your business. You didn't go or couldn't go to the bank because you were too young and they said you just got in business or you didn't have enough credit established or maybe even what they would deem as bad credit.

Don't let those things deter you from starting your business. One of the most amazing things that I benefited from when I went to chiropractic school and where I was chosen and where I chose to attend chiropractic school was, they had a concept of a home-based business. So, then that way all of your bills, if you think about it, are cut in half. I was privileged to have my rent and all other expenses.

In my case, I didn't have rent because I owned the combined building, but you can have the building that you practice or service individuals out of or maybe just a room in the rear of the building that can be used for you and your family's quiet space, where you reduce your expenses so that you can survive in business. We only had one light bill, water bill, gas bill or phone or Internet service.

You want to make sure that you are reducing your bills and your expenses to give yourself the time necessary to sustain yourself. You may need approximately six months. You just may have to open longer operational hours or work at your job a little while longer or start work somewhere else to give your business enough time to get the clients to where it can sustain itself, but do not be in fear of the fact that you can't do it.

You just have to do what works for you. You have to tighten the belt. You have to not get caught up in what everyone else is doing or how everyone else was living or what loan someone else may have had or what some family member may or may not have given them. And you have to get started with the tools that you have to run your business and in time you will be exactly where you see yourself in your mind. Just get started and pick that location.

Location, location, location has been a thing that I have heard.

Location is critical.

Chapter 6:
Build It and They Will Come

Main Principle

Building a business and laying out a blueprint are both imperative. After reducing it to paper and laying it out, the other part of building it and they will come is providing that service to the clients or customers that you desire.

In the previous chapter, we talked about rolling our sleeves up and getting to it...picking a location. So, we should have a sense of the location that you desire. A mental picture of where you want to start your business. We have talked about in the previous sections.

By now, you know we should have taken a look into the local government and whether certain occupational facility or service licenses were required. Also, you should have taken a visit online to www.irs.gov and decided on whether or not to apply for your tax ID number as well as if you're going to incorporate or operate a sole proprietorship.

You've decided whether or not to use your own social security number. You have also decided on and know firmly what your business name is by now.

Just think about it.

Six chapters ago, you were not even here. You should have a fire and desire burning inside of you. I know that there was a night that you did not go to sleep because you were just tossing and turning and so many things were running through your mind.

Guess what? Been there, done that.

I want to tell you something, when those ideas run through your mind, write them down immediately. There is a quote from a spiritual standpoint that says, "Write the vision down and make it plain" and there is a tremendous amount of truth to that.

In this chapter, "Build it and They will Come," now we have the location, at least if nothing else in our mind of where we want to be. Now, it's time for you to do your layout on how you want your business to be set up and structured. How you want it to flow.

You want to think about where you want your staff to be. Where do you want your lobby or sitting area to be? For example, if it's a restaurant, you want to know how you want your chairs positioned. Other things to consider, where do you want your wash station? How many restrooms will you have? What things are you're going to place in the restrooms? Will you have a laundry station?

If you are someone who is in the health industry, maybe you will have certain examination rooms and you want to know how you're going to position the individuals in the room. What décor will you put on the walls? Which direction may the doors open? You need to put that layout to paper and if it's already on paper and you've already chosen your location, you already know by now how you're going to lay that business out because you've chosen that location or you walking through it and you're getting your ideas.

So, lay it out in your mind, but the important factor that I do want you to understand and get, not only in this situation, but in life. You want to make sure that you're never static. You want to be fluid. You want to be able to move and flex and be pliable and able to move and work in certain situations. That doesn't mean that you just have to deal with what you have that's been given to you per se or just quote unquote, "just make things work," but at the same time, you can have a vision in your head and hold it so strong as someone near and dear to you, but don't sweat the small stuff. Get going. Get the vision. Work at making it move because your first location may just be that..... your first location.

Building a business and laying out a blueprint are both imperative. First and foremost, the blueprint is necessary so that you know once you're going to do some type of conceptual idea. Some people, when you ask them, "what do you want to do?" They respond, "I want to start a business." Well, how do you want your business to operate? They get silent because they haven't given much thought to it.

And after giving it thought, you must act. After reducing it to paper and laying it out, the other part of building it and they will come is you providing that service to the individuals, parishioners, patrons, clients, customers, etc. that you desire. Focus on giving them a quality product. Focus on serving them as if they are your only customer. Focus on treating them like you want to be treated. Focus on them as if they are the only thing that matters. Focus on them as if your life depended on it. Focus on them as if you don't want them to go to anyone else to seek what you have because they know that you are undoubtedly the qualified person or persons out there and they won't even begin to think about going anywhere else because you have built their trust in the manner at which you operate and conduct your business. So, build it. The time it takes to build it, build it, and I guarantee you this, THEY WILL COME.

I don't want to sound monotonous, but you know what I'm going to say. It's not about being different, but what we have in this book. For the person that reads this book, you know that it's different. By now, if you're in chapter six, you know that this book is different from anything that's out there because we're talking to you. We're walking with you and guiding you step by step to get you to a different place.

> **"Focus on serving them as if they are your only customer."**
>
> Dr. Zeboye A. Doctor

Currently, we're on the sixth step and we have nine more steps to go and we're going to climb those steps together. I'm going to climb them with you. I'm going to come back down from my top step down and I'm down on the step right now where you are because I have been there and I want you to take the steps. I want you to graduate from the steps. I even want you to descend back down to the steps, as necessary, to build your foundation and get you where you want to go and also help someone else to get where you are or where you have been because of this book.

Being different... marketing as it is works on the mental. This is a psychological tool that is used to attract, influence, persuade, even intimidate; place fear; detour individuals. You just have to decide on what side you want to be on.

You just have to decide on what you want your clients to say about you. Forget about what everybody else is doing and find out what works for you. Remember when you made up in your mind at one point that you wanted this and not that. Remember that feeling and remember what you said that you were going to do and not do. Remember that.

Now we all grow and evolve throughout time, but the core of who and what we are and our vision, that is not going to change. That is to provide a better life for ourselves, our family, friends, and serve humanity. And once you do those things, the compensation is going to come. No ifs, ands or buts about it.

So, stick to what you see in your mind and what resonates and moves with you and in doing so people are going to come and seek your counsel and advice; maybe taste your food or drink your beverages or seek your business for rest and relaxation or entertainment or spiritual guidance and support. Whatever arena you're in. The marketing aspect is how you put and portray yourself out there to others and the best tool that I have found more than anything is referrals, but you have to serve and take care of your people, your patients, your clients in order for them to refer the people that you desire.

And if you find yourself not attracting what you desire, then listen to me and listen to me very well. You should step back and evaluate what you need to do or not do in order to attract the clientele or have the business that you desire.

Market, market in the right places.

Market the truth.

Market the truth.

Market the TRUTH.

I know that in this society it is very tough because when you feel that you tell people the truth; you show them this and that and they don't receive it and other people are doing this, that and the other and they're flocking over there to them. Listen, the majority of the people on our planet are misinformed about all areas of everything that they know about and what they don't know about. As I said before, that you have heard, "to whom much is given, much is required. You be the one. You be that different one. You be that person that's going to give them an experience that they have never experienced and they will come and they will also bring others.

As they said, Rome was not built in a day.

I like to say that the pyramids were not built in a day, but as you look at that marvel or those marvels, they have stood and are standing the test of time because of the integrity, the passion, the spirituality, the knowledge, the motivation, the commitment, the dedication, the sacrifice, and the wherewithal of the ancestors who build them. They are still standing because of the foundation, not just the one they were built upon, but the core of the individuals. That building, it speaks to what they really are truly marvelous, marvelous structures. This concludes chapter six of the book and we will journey with you to chapter seven.

Chapter 7:

Who's Going to Do the Work?

Main Principle
You're the one that's going to do the work. You have to put that sweat in.

The main idea of this chapter is to get the reader to understand that now that you have built or chosen a location; you have your company name; the tax id number, your occupational, service or facility license. Now, you have think about hiring employees or independent contractors. Will you build your team, sub-contract or outsource? Or on the other hand, if you have the sole proprietorship, you are the one that's doing the work yourself. Now, you have to decide.

A lot of businesses, particularly the individuals that I am speaking to and was motivated to write this book for are doing most, if not, all of the work. Yes...You're the one that's going to do the work. You've already answered that question, but that may just be in the beginning.

You must look ahead down the road and think about the time where you're just going to have to come to a point that you're going to have to hire your help. And the successful businesses that are out there. Some of the greatest business owners that are out there, they are great, in my opinion, because they are successful at duplicating themselves. They are successful at finding out what they don't know or realizing what they don't know and finding someone to assist them and what they don't know and filling the void in what they have in their business.

They are great at noticing that their business is lacking something and they're going to work to go and get it.

You have to put that sweat in. You have to think about efficiency. You have to decide on whether or not you're going to work just a few hours a day. You've got to decide on whether you're going to work an eight-hour shift or maybe 12-hour shifts or 16 hours or maybe you're going to be the business that never closes.

> **"You have to put that sweat in. You have to think about the work that has to be done and who's going to do it."**
>
> Dr. Zeboye A. Doctor

But, you have to think about the work that has to be done and who's going to do it based upon the resources that you may or may not have available to you. And if you're that aspiring business owner or entrepreneur that may be a sole proprietor or you're incorporated and you're the only person or employee of the business, all the work that needs to be done has to be done by you. So, you must make sure that you do not spread yourself thin and take on more things than what you can handle.

You must work to balance all that you have going on in your life. You may be a business owner, but I am sure that you have a family in some way, shape, form or fashion. In the previous chapters you've heard me speak on TIME. Giving things time. Sometimes in this society that we are in, the quest for greatness gets us off balance. But, we must make time even if it is one day a week for family.

Chapter 8:
Getting and Making Cheddar

Main Principle

There must be an evolution in the way that you deal with yourself and others. You must learn how to manage, spend, grow, and acquire money.

Show Me the Money

Putting money in its proper place is extremely important for your company. At this point, the reader must decide on how they are going to hold, grow, and transfer money necessary to run their business. And this step is a very important step. Some of the individuals may decide to hold, secure, and provide safety to their own money. Others may want a warranty, security or protection for their money. So, they may decide to go and open up a banking account, which would consist of a checking and savings account for their business.

Or if you are sole proprietor, you could open up a personal checking account. So, in order to open your business account, you must have the Articles of Incorporation from the secretary of state, which you should already have by now. You will also need to have your tax identification number that you obtain from the Internal Revenue Service. As a result of the acts that were perpetrated by individuals on September 11, 2001. additional forms of documentation are now needed to open up a bank account.

For example, bills to prove one's residence or location, driver's license, passports, military identification or your own identity or whomever may be opening the account that has been given the power to open the account and conduct and transact business for the company.

The uniqueness about this idea that aspiring business owners should know is that you're going to have to keep records. Having a bank account is one way in which you can keep up with your financial records because in most cases the way that you're going to transact business is to write a check to other business owners,

"Putting capital in its proper place is extremely important in your company."

Dr. Zeboye A. Doctor

vendors or companies in which you have expenses with that are necessary for operating your business. You may also use a debit or check card for transacting business.

Your business and that information is going to be needed in order to conduct business rather than utilizing cash. When using cash, the paper trail that may be needed to adequately protect and give you the deductions and credits necessary when it's time to prepare your taxes may become cumbersome if you're not using a system that can be readily tracked as is necessary in order to track the spending habits of your company, determine the expenses of your company, and the tax liability that is necessary for your company.

The business account can also show the growth of your company because of the positive or black status, that your account is in and may continue to soar in as you become more efficient at operating your company. When opening your business accounts, you may want to not only have one checking account for the business, but also an operating account. You may want to decide to have an operating account in which the monthly expenses that are necessary to run your business will be held until needed.

Additionally, you may even decide to have an account where you deposit money that will go towards paying your taxes such as your property taxes, tangible taxes, federal income taxes, employment taxes, etc.

You may even want to have an account to be able to set money aside for a "rainy day" for the company or where you can began to put the company's wealth so that it is not readily assessable to you or others in order to help with your sustainability by not keeping it all in one location and this type of discipline is not only recommended, but it's necessary. Here me when I say NECESSARY.

Because depending on how much your company generates, the bank or the FDIC may only insure you up to $250,000 per account and that information you may want to conduct additional research on as to the rules and regulations surrounding your assets.

In the words of the late Notorious B.I.G., "more money, more problems," and he didn't necessarily mean it like that, but as we've said before, "to whom much is given, much is required." In order to get to that place that you desire to be in your business, there has to be an evolution in your thought process. There must be an evolution in the way that you deal with yourself and others. You must learn how to manage, spend, grow, and acquire money.

All successful people and successful businesses have knowledge of this. And this is not an area at which you can avoid, but expect to become successful and have a successful, vital, vibrant, and financially sustainable company.

Chapter 9:
Spreading the Word

Main Principle
"You have to decide on what you want to do towards making your business grow."

This chapter provides the reader with some ideas and concepts that they may want to evaluate when marketing their business. The reader must decide how they are going to inform the misinformed, uninformed consumer or potential client to the industry of work that they have decided to enter, serve the community, and engage in.

Chapter 9 gives a glimpse into different avenues in which the reader may want to consider that they may have not previously thought about in order to make their business grow. That may be already being utilized by them, just maybe in a different manner; maybe for a different purpose or that they may just not know exists because they may not operate in that realm of reality. But, they may need to because it may be very effective for spreading the word about the industry that they are engaged in.

> **"You're going to have to decide on how you're going to market your business."**

As a business owner or aspiring business owner, you're going to have to decide on how you're going to market your business. You may want to decide to inform individuals about the location of your business through magazines, press releases or newspapers. You may also consider some advertisements, marketing on radio stations, and television commercials. You may even decide to look into the booming thing in this industry right now, which is social media (e.g., Facebook, Instagram, Twitter, LinkedIn, etc.), which it seems that so many Americans are just giving all of their life, effort and energy to.

You know, it's not uncommon.

In fact, it's very, very common to observe individuals on Facebook, Instagram, Twitter, just strolling through their phones, tablets, desktop computers, and laptops. You know, so much time, effort, and energy is lost in companies on individuals doing their job at work because a lot of the employees are surfing the Internet or looking at the things that they want to consume while they should be working to help their employer's business succeed.

So, you have to decide on what method you may want to use in order to attract new business, if not all available.

Another idea that you may want to consider is billboard advertisement, websites, and generating an email account to build your customer base, if you are a sole proprietor or even for your company. There are various companies that you could take a look at such as GoDaddy, Host Gator, just to name a couple. You can also research different internet providers that have business emails that you purchase for your company. All of that comes and has to be decided for the individual that seeks to start and open a business in this era. Some people may just decide to take the traditional route and focus on word of mouth for one avenue exclusively.

And if that's what you desire because you have your plan figured out and you know where you want to be, that's perfectly fine. But, I do not want you to discount either one of those arenas nor am I telling you to go and get involved in all of those arenas or that one arena is any more particular than the other.

One thing about advertisement that I have discovered in business is that it can be very costly. Another thing that I have found out personally regarding advertisement is that initially I didn't want to advertise because of the dogma that I had come into about just having a referral-based business. But the truth of the matter of it is how will individuals know that you're out there and have a business if you don't do some form of advertisement.

> **"Some form or multiple forms of marketing are going to have to be tested in order for your business to be effective."**
>
> Dr. Zeboye A. Doctor

There is a quote that says, "Bad news travels faster than good news."

Well, what if you're doing a good thing? What if you're not doing anything thing, quote on quote bad? Your information may still get out there a little slower than others. You don't want to exclusively depend on word of mouth in marketing your vision where you desire for it to be. So, you're going to have to put some of your income that you generate from your business back into marketing and that may be 10%, 20% or 30% of what the business generates.

But, ultimately you have to decide on what you want to do towards making your business grow. Another factor that you have to decide upon and look at how your business is being generated. What arena is responsible for helping your office and business sustain itself? And that is the first area that you need to work to continue to give back to, to continue to feed it so that it continues to help your business and your vision achieve that return on the investment (ROI).

But, undoubtedly, some form or multiple forms of marketing are going to have to be investigated and tested in order for your business to be effective. You may employ the aid of a marketing company. You may know a friend or family member that has experience in that particular arena. So, seek the counsel of someone that has some knowledge on what you are interested in. From there, work to make the decision on the arena you really want to investigate or maybe even stay away from. But, be willing and open to trying the marketing avenues.

There is one lesson that I want to share with you that I learned the hard way about marketing. Marketing does NOT guarantee you any business. Marketing does NOT guarantee to give you that which you put back in.

"Everything takes TIME."

There is a component that we have discussed in prior chapters about that it's necessary in everything that we do. One word, four letters, and it starts with a "T."

It's called TIME.

Everything takes time.

And now that I've been in business for 11 years, the thing that I realized a few years ago is that marketing only gives individuals and awareness about who you are and what you have to offer. It does not guarantee that individuals are going to come to you, but do not be discouraged and fear marketing because of that. Because the one thing that you do need to know, that you gain from marketing, is the sense of individuals discovering who you are and what you have to offer.

And in that, coupled with time, you will begin to see that the marketing arena that you are a paying that dividend to, it is going to pay off. The question is how effective and what that return on investment will be. That is why some individuals may do a little bit of everything to market their businesses. So, remember marketing doesn't guarantee you a certain amount of money or certain business. What you put your marketing to; the arena that you placed it in, it guarantees you the publicity that your business exist and you are out there.

Chapter 10:
Polishing Up Your Skills

Throughout this particular chapter, it is important that the readers understand, know, and also put in the effort necessary in making their business better. In every industry, there is a lot of information that changes the new innovative ideas that are out there in individual industries. And in fact, there is just some information that every person in their respective industry, just did not learn and whatever school of thought that they are engaged in. But, once you find out that information or come to the knowledge of it, then you must make a decision on whether or not to add this information to your business or help your overall model for success.

In addition to that, this is a nice, great opportunity for you to evaluate your structure as far as the ideas you have coming to you and accepting those as your own and whether or not you might need to let go of certain ideas, misconceptions or false perceptions that you may have had because you see that it may not be working out. And that's also a great quality of a great leader as a business owner.

You may even find out what things are working; what things are not working; and you add or take away those ideas, philosophies, actions, items, etc. from the business or adding to the business as necessary in order to propel you to the next level so that you do not become stagnant so that you retain the quality that you desire and even elevate, most importantly, to the next level in your business/ professional growth.

The thing that I noticed from my experiences in business and also just my investigation is that, you know, there is a total picture to all of this. Technically, there is not a right or wrong way to do anything. I had a quote that I used to use when I was a teacher about 16 years ago and it was, "if you don't plan to succeed, then you're planning to fail. One way or the other, you are planning for something."

So, as you're going through your business and your business begins to show you certain signs of success or distress; certain red flags or things that need to be attended to, do not wait until the situation gets out of control or you're critical in order to address, change or alter the situation or issue that is presented. When you see it, you want to deal with it as swiftly as you can so that the morale, the culture, the environment, but most importantly, the business in and of itself does not suffer a blow and not be able to recover.

> **"If you don't plan to succeed, then you're planning to fail. One way or the other, you are planning for something."**
>
> Dr. Zeboye A. Doctor

There are several ways that you can polish your skills. For example, there may be continual education requirements or certain seminars that you can attend as a business owner and learn more about your particular industry that you are engaged in. So, attending those seminars may enable you to gain a wealth and plethora of knowledge from individuals from different walks of life. A lot of them may attempt to sell you something. So, you have to be very conscious of what to buy. Do not be an impulse buyer. Step back away from a situation and make the decision as you feel necessary.

Listen to Yourself

You know, sometimes you just have to follow your gut and listen to what your gut is telling you or your spirit is telling you. But, as a great tool in business, I have begun to learn that I make no hasty decisions right away as though I will not have an opportunity in the future.

One thing about marketing that individuals or sales people do and that is they appeal to emotions. They appeal to ignorance. They appeal to you being a novice or new in the industry. Be careful about that. People may try to make you all type of promises about this, that and the other.

> **"Listen to your inner most being and what is going on."**
>
> Dr. Zeboye A. Doctor

If it smells like a rat, then it's a rat.

If it sounds a little funny, more than likely, it is.

Listen to your inner most being and what is going on. Adopt that you do not make a decision spontaneously or on impulse, unless your life depends on it. Step away from the situation. There was a book that I read about a very wealthy man in Babylon and I learned a lot in that book about making decisions and the importance of being rational. You want to be rational.

Don't allow anyone to try and dictate a decision to you or based upon the particular situation that may or may not be presented itself.

Another thing that you can do outside of continuing education courses or seminars is to conduct professional development workshops or staff meetings for you and your staff that you may have in your company. For example, weekly, monthly, yearly meetings and even daily meetings before or after the business day. These kinds of meetings are important to keep morale up. You want to at least make sure you're meeting with your team at least once a month. And even once a month can be a stretch because depending on how big your company is or when you're starting out, you may need to be meeting weekly and if nothing else, talking to certain individuals, depending on the structure of your company daily so that situations do not get out of hand.

As your company grows and develops, income generated, expenses increase, different people are coming in, even inventory, things can become overwhelming for you and you may begin to delegate to others. That's when money can come up missing. That's when people, clients, customers, and employees taking inventory home for their own personal usage. You know, you have to be conscious of those things. You know, you may or may not decide to have uniforms and badges for your staff. You may even cover the cost of it initially. But, I tell you this while I'm on that topic, consider name badges for your employees rather than stitched, personalized items in the clothing so that uniforms can transfer over to someone else if that individual does not work out.

And it's not that you are thinking about someone failing. What you're doing from a business standpoint and a business owner standpoint is working to make what you have stretch because you may go through a 90-day probationary period with the individual and before the 90 days are up, you may decide that you might not want them. You've taken the time, effort energy, and money in utilizing the resources to make that person look the way that you desire them to in order for them to represent your brand, but they just may not fit your mold and you have to make the decision swiftly to move on before that person jeopardizes your vision.

You can't be afraid to make those decisions. Things or situations may come up where you may be slow to make a decision; but, you know that you have to make it. However, you must be calculated; be calm, but do not allow what we've discussed in previous chapters to rise up. Do not let fear make you move. Don't think about if you're being stubborn, just think about whether an individual does or does not fit the mold for your business and don't be afraid to let that person go if they are not "fitting the mold." That's why interviewing individuals before you hire them is very, very important, including your own family, so that people get an understanding of your expectations. That's how you want to polish up on your skills.

Polish up on yourself, being a business owner.

Polish up on yourself at going to the next level. That's how you want to do that.

There was a spiritual advisor that I had while I was going through chiropractic school. He said that "roses grow in the midst of trash and you might say, well, what did he mean by that? Well, I will tell you. What I gathered from it was that even in the midst of trash or a dump, there is fertilizer, nutrients, water, etc. that is in that trash that will allow that rose to grow and out of your situation, out of your circumstance, you can grow into that which you desire and see yourself becoming.

> **"You must be willing to put in the hard work, dedication, and sacrifice necessary in order for you to become that which you see yourself becoming in your mind."**
>
> Dr. Zeboye A. Doctor

Just remember, you must be persistent. You must be consistent. You must be willing to put in the hard work, dedication, and sacrifice necessary in order for you to become that which you see yourself becoming in your mind. By now, I know that these suggestions outlined in this book are taking root. It is taking form and there has been a manifestation, although you may say small, in your life. There has been a transformation in your life through the process of reading this book. You have been enlightened. But again, this information does absolutely no good whatsoever unless, unless you began to apply it.

Chapter 11:

Forming Your Inner Circle

Main Principle
You cannot do this on your own. It takes an entire community to sustain one or more businesses.

The main focus of Chapter 11 is to get the reader to understand that you cannot do this on your own. No individual is on an island. There is a quote that says, "it takes a whole village to raise a child." It takes an entire community to sustain a business or businesses. So, no one person will be the sole responsible party for the success of your company.

Not even YOU.

It's because of the people that you are serving. Notice that I said the people or the clients that you have that you are and will continue to experience the success that you are experiencing. So, you must form your circle. No if, ands or buts about it. If you are in the healthcare industry and in my case, you are a Chiropractor. Some individuals may want to limit you to strictly being a back doctor and it's nothing wrong with that. Go with me for a second.

A monkey does not know that it is a monkey. It's just what others have called it. Be careful what you allow others to call you. In that, taking it a bit further, it is what you respond to. In building your network, if they want to think of you as the "neck and back pain" doctor, you have to learn to deal with individuals where they are until you can put them on the level where you desire for them to be. For example, if you are formulating a circle and someone is responsible for the neck and the back, allow that to be you. Someone has to take care of the ears, nose, and the throat. Somebody may be the Cardiologist; another person may be the Kidney Specialist or Pulmonary Specialist. Someone else may be the Neurologist.

Everybody has their role in making the human body what it is in this healthcare industry.

Everyone has a ROLE.

In forming your circle, make sure that you identify individuals that are on equal or greater footing as yourself, whether it be financially, socially or spiritually. Make sure you surround yourself with individuals who you desire to go and grow with you. Individuals that want, in action, for you to go and grow with them as well. Because oftentimes, people may see you for what you are doing and want to attach to your success. You are an up and coming business owner. So, a lot of people are going to try to be a part of your circle.

You have to ask yourself two questions: 1) Do I want them to be a part of my circle? 2) Do I want to become a part of their circle? And if the answer is NO, get up and move immediately. One or two things are going to happen that I've found out and that is "If you are not pushing me forward, you are holding me back." And you must decide which position you want to be in.

If you are always pushing someone else, whose pushing you?

If you are always holding someone else, whose holding you?

As previously stated, there must be a balance in our personal, physical, spiritual, social, financial, economic, and professional growth. There must be a balance. You must associate yourself with individuals of the same like minds and mental capacity. If you don't, it will become very draining or exhausting. This is something that you already know, which is why you decided to pick up this book and why you're reading this chapter because you have identified with the truth that we have put before you and you desire to know more.

Remember, you must not use this book to simply keep your time or for information purposes only. You must apply the content of this book in order for it to manifest itself in your life. So, begin to form your circle. Who is your personal banker or financial advisor? Who takes care of the maintenance of your car? Who is the individual that takes care of repairs in your home? Who is your spiritual advisor? Who is the person responsible for your grooming and clothing? Who takes care of the business marketing and apparel, information brochures, pamphlets, etc. for your business? Where do you purchase your stationary equipment? Where do you shop for your food?

Every single aspect of your being MUST, undoubtedly, work to be with individuals that help to build and sustain you, your network, and your community. Your community where you live, work, and play should be comprised of individuals that think like you or it should be going into the direction of those that think like you.

Your community looks like it does because of what you are putting into or NOT putting into it. What you are giving or NOT giving to it. What you are taking to or taking away from it. You are directly responsible for how your community looks.

If you do not like the way that your community looks, build your network to change it. And if you build your network to change it, your business is going to be directly impacted from it directly.

In closing of this chapter, remember you need a network, community, affiliation, assimilation of individuals with like minds. You need people that will say that they are going to help you sustain YOU and YOUR VISION and you're going to have to go to individuals that are going to sustain your vision. You should strongly consider, think, ponder, and then

> **"Be careful what you allow others to call you AND what you respond to."**
>
> Dr. Zeboye A. Doctor

act on whether or not the place that you're eating at is going to come and utilize your services. If not, you need to re-evaluate that relationship. In life, there are some people that you may not be able to get around dealing with. But, you should never stop focusing to find individuals to comprise your network where you and your network can sustain itself in the community.

If you define the word "network," your body is a network. If you look up "community," your body is a community. If you research the meaning of system, it is comprised of one thing communicating with multiple things for the benefit of the entire whole, part or thing. That is what a successful business is comprised of. This is also the characteristics of your business and is not any different from any other successful business. You must have these essential parts.

Your inner circle may be comprised of individuals from your social and spiritual organizations. It could be you going out to other business owners and talking with them about whether or not they have other networks and work to form a network with them. It may very well be you going to speak with other business owners and expressing to them "Hey, I have a business in the area and I've decided to come and check out your business and support you financially and in action. So, what I'm looking for is for you and your business to come and actively support me and my business as I've come to actively support and feed you and your family." Challenge those businesses, business owners, staff, etc. Work to offer them a discount for the services you offer for coming and supporting your business in order for your business to sustain itself. But, remember, as with networking and anything else, IT TAKES TIME. Do not be discouraged about someone not coming to you immediately, next week or even next month.

Make sure that you are careful in spending your money, treasure, and resources wisely. Be conscious of that because if you are depleting yourself; your resources or your well and your well is not being filled up as fast as you are depleting it, then just maybe you're putting your resources in the wrong place. And before the situation becomes critical, as we've stated before, "A wise and great business owner will correct a situation before it becomes critical" or to the point where the sustainability is severely jeopardized and cannot recover.

"Life does not give you everything you ask for, but it will give you what you put your thoughts and actions towards most." Form your network. Form your company, but most importantly, form YOU.

> **"Life does not give you everything you ask for, but it will give you what you put your thoughts and actions towards most."**
>
> Dr. Zeboye A. Doctor

Chapter 12:

The Safety Net

Main Principle
Every company functioning at maximum efficiency or those who may be even operating on a thread have policies and procedures in place.

The goal of Chapter 12 is to emphasize the importance of policies and procedures. In order to have a successful company, policies and procedures are essential.

Every company functioning at maximum efficiency or those who may be even operating on a thread have policies and procedures in place. The difference between the efficient company or high efficiency company versus that which is not as efficient or that which may be on life support is the presence of policies and procedures that are not only verbally communicated, but they are also written and in place for anyone that is involved with the day-to-day operations of the company to locate. They know what they are. They can put their hands on them, but most importantly, they utilize the policies or procedures day in and day out that are responsible for the success of the company.

Policies and procedures are as simple as opening and closing procedures in your business. How you want every single person that is responsible for opening and/or closing the company for the business day to operate. These policies and procedures need to be reduced to writing. For instance, procedures for whoever the responsible person is for opening the business, it may be unlocking the door; disarming the alarm system; turning on the ventilation system or air conditioning unit for the company. It may be turning on the computers and allowing them to boot up. It could be opening up the window blinds or making sure that the trash cans are empty. It may be assuring that the bathrooms are in functioning and working order. Also, walking throughout the business to make sure that the company has not been vandalized the night before.

The responsible person can check the email system for emails or the phone systems for voice messages. It may be checking the local U.S. postal mail for incoming or outgoing mail. It can be tasks as simple as making sure that the laundry from the previous day has been completed (washed, folded, and restocked in the storage place) or needs to be completed for that day. It can be bills going out; taking inbound calls and communicating with clients or staff from another company. They may be making outbound calls on old accounts or previous debt that may be outstanding.

> **"In order to have a successful company, policies and procedures are essential."**
>
> Dr. Zeboye A. Doctor

Policies and procedures cannot be over emphasized. For example, if you are in the restaurant industry and you make coffee, whatever procedure you follow for making a batch of coffee, that needs to be written down so that anyone, that you have entrusted with making your coffee, makes your coffee the same way, every single time that it is made. It may be checking a client in to your automotive center. You need to make sure that the same procedure is adhered to every single time that a client comes in to have their car serviced. It may be cleaning your bathrooms. There should be a checklist in your bathroom.

Have you ever gone to a gas station or some restaurant and they have a bathroom log? That log is there because that business owner knows that staff may become involved and so entrenched in the day-to-day operations that they may forget to clean the restroom. And we all have gone to a restroom while traveling on the road and saw one that you did not even want to step foot in and breathe in, let alone void. But, the successful companies that you think of that have the restrooms that you would not mind stopping to at any given time, they have those facilities in the manner that you identify with that sets with you that way because they pay attention to it and they know that their company's success is directly connected to how that restroom looks.

So, as a business owner, if you have a childcare center, you want to make sure that the areas that are pertinent to the success of your company thriving are well managed accordingly. And no one area should be no greater than the other because if it's in your business, all of it is important to the success of your business. If it's not, get rid of it because it's a distraction to your business. So, if it's in your business, there should be a policy and procedure in place for communicating with your staff and patrons of your business if you desire for it to be successful.

You don't have to reinvent the wheel.

Fall back on your training, maybe a company that you were previously a part of that system works. Fall back on that training. If the enterprise that you have been employed by in the past had policies and procedures that worked because more than likely that's common information, reflect back on those procedures and use it as a framework to develop your own system. But, check and make sure that it's common information that can be utilized in your business and you're not taking someone else's intellectual property as if it were your own.

You need policies and procedures in place and your staff needs to know where to obtain certain supplies or materials essential for the success of the business. Reduce that to writing. Start comprising that information and putting it in a book and that will form your manual. You need a manual on how to run your business so that if an individual on your staff has a question, the first thing that you should ask them is "have you referred to the manual?" And the one thing that they should know is to refer to the manual and look it up.

If your staff is coming to you and asking you questions over and over and over again that you have put in your manual, maybe you should evaluate that person's role in your company. If you are being asked or made aware of a situation time and time and time and time again and you have not reduced it to writing, you must question your role as the leader of that company and not reducing that information to writing. It needs to be in your manual if it is coming up time and time and time again.

If you find yourself asking and answering and doing the same things over and over and over again, that is part of your office's standard operating procedures and it needs to be reduced to writing and placed in the manual so that when you hire new employees or you have someone that's going through the 90-day probationary period or the first day you meet them and give them a job, you hand them these resources and say, "this is the manual for conducting business in our office. If you want to know how to answer the phone, I'm going to go over that with you, but this is the way that you answer the phone in the office." If you don't give them an example, they will began to fall back on only what they know and that behavior will become a part of your business if you don't give them an example. The one thing that I have and do not hold anyone that's a part of my business responsible or and accountable for is anything that I have not taught them.

However, what I will hold them accountable for is everything that I have shown them and not adhering to the manual that is in place because I tell them. I go over it with them and make them accountable to that manual. Also, I let them know that if a situation arises that is not something that I have taught them, they are to bring it to my attention immediately and let me address the matter. They are to only deal with the responsibilities they have been entrusted with and what has been laid upon them based upon the scope of their employment. They do not, under any circumstances, operate outside of that.

Business owners, you must stress this with your employees as well and if they operate outside of what you have in place, there is a structure in place, whether it be an oral or verbal reprimand. Whether it be the magnitude where there is a written reprimand along with that. If the conduct and behavior or action is so detrimental to the company and the sustainability of your business, it may be immediate termination. If you, as the business owner, don't deal with it in those stages, those individuals that have been hired are agents of your corporation. They are an extension of you as the owner of that corporation and any and all actions of your agent. You as the business owner or the business may be directly responsible for the actions of the agents. So, I implore you not to bring on or hire individuals as a part of your corporation that are inadequate or unqualified.

I have tried it. I have been there. I have done that. It does not end the way that you think it is going to end in your irrational mind to bring them apart of your corporation. In your rational mind, you know that they're not qualified. You know that they are inadequate. You know that they have not been trained and you know that you should not bring them on and let them free to be apart and operate in your business because they have not been trained properly. Do not make that mistake because it can become costly.

I like to say that in running or operating a business, you want to make sure that you tell your staff that the tools and information that they gain from being a part of your business, they can apply those directly to their day-to-day life. You know, routines, habits, rituals or just down, ok, "this is just the way that we do it." There is absolutely nothing wrong with those things. Just make sure that if this is down right, "just the way that you do it," that you reduce it to writing so that other individuals know. And when you reduce it to writing, you are creating your paper trail to show that this is the way that you conduct business. So, if anyone steps outside of that, although you may not be absolved of any responsibilities of your agents, you can note that those were the grounds at which you released that person from being a part of your business or terminated them.

> **"Write the vision down and make it plain. You won't regret it."**
>
> Dr. Zeboye A. Doctor

If by now you haven't started your business, start by writing policies and procedures in your home on how to clean the home. If you have kids or family members, write down those things to let individuals know that this is how you clean the tub. This is how you clean the shower. This is how you clean the toilet. This is how you mop the floor. This is how you wipe down the walls. This is how you wash and dry the dishes. This is how you clean the living room. Those small policies and procedures and ways or modus operandi of doing things in the home can translate right over to the business. On the otherhand, if you are in an industry right now that you are considering spinning off of because you have the knowledge base and you want to duplicate the service, think about some of the policies and procedures that you may have right now that are in place and work to adopt those as your own and making you successful as an individual, business owner, and as a leader and pillar in the community.

Play it safe. Write the vision down and make it plain. You won't regret it.

Chapter 13:

Who's Going to Pay for This

Main Principle

Focus on what you have and put in the work and sacrifice as needed until you get what you don't have.

This particular chapter is going to delve into HOW to fund your vision. There are multiple ways in which one may seek to fund their business. I'll just go ask someone in my family. Someone else might say, "Well, I don't have that option." Another person may even say, "Let me go to the bank and get a loan." Well, a business line of credit or line of credit is not out of the question. A line of credit on a startup business and if you have never been in business or filed a business return will in most cases be based upon your personal credit score.

If you are a person who recently graduated and received a certification from some type of institution or program and you are new to all of this and as some would say "wet behind the ears" or "green as a blade of grass," then, this may not be your best route for you at this time for various reasons. You haven't been in business long enough. You don't have at least two years of tax returns, which most bank institutions are going to ask for or you may not have the work history there to prove in your past work experiences that will necessitate the bank

---

approving you the desired loan amount because you have just completed school. But, don't be discouraged by this.

The bank institutions are there for one purpose and one purpose only and this is to make money. Do not be deceived. They are to balance their risk and the chances of them making a profit against every account holder in their institution. If you don't fit the mold for the ideal person to lend money to or you don't know someone at the bank, chances are you're not going to get a loan, but it's okay. That doesn't mean that you give up and not apply. They may ask you to put together a business plan and research can be performed on a business plan as it pertains to the line or industry in which you are engaged in.

Who is your target market?

What is the predicted income?

What is the average income for someone starting a business?

The money that you would need for a building, if you decided to pick a location that may have been great, but it still needs to be build out to suit your needs?

The bank will lend you money based upon your credit worthiness and also the risk that they're willing to take in your individual market.

When I first began in business, I put together a business plan, but someone else used that business plan to procure the loan at a lending institution based upon their relationship. I wasn't able to get the loan because I did not have the work history, the credit or a family member there that was willing to cosign. So, what I did, and as stated in the previous chapter, I'm thankful for my lessons that I learned at Sherman College and the environment that was cultivated at Sherman, which was to start your own business from home or have a home-based business. As discussed in the previous chapters, in that way you, will have one set of bills for home and work. You want to really, really investigate this option.

You may have to start your business from your home that you presently reside in and build up your clientele to a point where you can afford to be in a stand-alone facility. Now, someone may be saying at this point, "I'm not going to have a home-based business. I'm not going to have people coming to my house." And this particular option may not be for you. But, before you eliminate this as an option, listen to the argument, think about it again. You develop one set of bills, thereby giving you more money to place in your pocket. You allow yourself to get to the point to where you can save, if you have not already saved or you can allow yourself to build a nest egg, if you are not privileged to have a family member that gave you a nest egg or has a nest egg that they will allow you to borrow from. Maybe the bank situation was your best route. So, you don't have to think about starting your business from home. But, for some people, starting a home-based business may be the only option available.

So, if you are a person who has your own trade license such as a cosmetologist or a barber, having a home-based business may not be a bad idea. If you're a person that wants to start a childcare facility, having a home-based business at first and dedicating certain areas of the home for business may not be a bad idea. You will have to check with that particular department in your city or state that oversees home-based businesses that to make sure that you're permitted by law.

But, don't exclude it without trying.

If you are an electrician, a carpenter, plumber or roofer, it's easy for you to start at home. You may even have your main office out of your car or truck. The key to it all is getting started. Having a vision, being dedicated to that vision and working up to the next best thing to get you closer to where you want to be.

Maybe you are a professional, such as a doctor or a lawyer, a home-based business may be well for you, if the other options are not plausible. One thing that you can consider as a professional is going to your clients until you can sustain a practice big enough to where that you can open up your own company or business as far as the physical location. That would definitely save you money. You can run your business out of your vehicle. You may have to visit different people's homes or their locations to see them, but you would not have the overhead that you would have by being in a stand-alone facility if the resources are not readily available.

> **"Don't allow fear and the lack of having something be the determinant or be the factor that discourages you from getting to where you see in your mind."**
>
> Dr. Zeboye A. Doctor

Again, don't allow fear and the lack of having something be the determinant or be the factor that discourages you from getting to where you see in your mind. As we've said before, "build it and they will come." If you build it, they will come, no if ands or buts about it.

I want to touch back on a previous point. Maybe you are a person that sells products, goods and services...maybe you can do business over the Internet. Maybe you desire a store and you could have the store out of your home and ship directly from your home to the customers that are in need of your services. Again, there is no right or wrong way of doing anything. Just work to hold your vision as close and as near and dear to you and go get it.

As previously stated, you may have to work on your job for a while in order to get the money and save up in order to start that business. You may want to go join the company of another or you and someone else, go into a business and start a partnership and you both equally share in the expense. Don't forget about what we said about that network in a previous chapter. You may want to network with some other individuals that are in a similar industry or an industry that compliments what you're offering that can help you and you guys can maybe share office space. The key is to get going. The key is to get started. Do not focus on what you do not have. Focus on what you do have.

"You can't get blood from a turnip" is one thing that I've been told, but you can look at your life and see what things or expenses that you have in your life that you can do without in order to allow your goal to become a reality. You can self-finance and start buying things right now, if you haven't done so already. Before I left Chiropractic school, I had enough equipment that I built or had built at the vocational colleges or schools near me that I had formed relationships with and I was ready to open the office. I even found furniture on the side of the road at a sale and used part of it to outfit my office. I had a plan to open my own business.

Hey, I have one even better. A 13-inch television that I bought my daughter 10 years prior to me opening my own business, I use that very same television in my lobby to get my office going. So, there are things that are in your home that people may have that are not making them any money or generating any revenue whatsoever. But I'll tell you this, once you decide to start your business, some of the very things that you thought cost you money can begin to generate you money because you have a license to do certain things. So, think about and focus on what you have and put in the work and sacrifice as needed until you get what you don't have. Don't focus on getting into more and more debt in order to finance your dreams. Don't make yourself a slave to debt.

I read a book that talked about having a "go to hell" clause and when you make yourself tied to the hip to someone or something that you might not want to be tied to as you grow and progress, it may not be so easy for you to separate yourself from that situation. So, you may want to go in with just the bare bones or necessities to get started so that you're not entrenched in that debt.

**"Don't focus on getting into more and more debt to finance your dreams.
Don't be a slave to debt."**

Chapter 14:
Much Needed Rest & Relaxation

Main Principle

If you work hard, be certain to play hard. The rest and relaxation are the rejuvenation to go back into your vision and make it better.

Chapter 14 emphasizes the importance of being sure to play hard after you've worked hard in your business. If you put your time, effort, and energy into working to make your business a successful company, you've got to put time, effort and energy into playing hard or what some may call, rest and relaxation.

Rest and relaxation is not just going home and going to sleep or going home and kicking your feet up on the sofa or the table; laying back in the recliner, watching TV. When you are a person that has your own business, when you have a vision, when you have a passion for something that means so much to you, at times you feel like you can keep going and going and going and going and going and you can. But, you must make time for rest and relaxation. You must make time to take yourself away from the business.

Rest and relaxation can be a fishing trip. It can be a get-away for the weekend. Your rest and relaxation can be in a lot of cases, depending on your industry, tied into the business. You go to a seminar or continuing education course and that's your get away from the normal day-to-day operations of your company. I remember the first time that I started in the business and I had to attend a continuing education course and I was looking at the chiropractic association's price for the continuing education courses. And I was new in the business and I'm saying, "Man, why are these people charging all this money?" When I looked at the hotel stay, they wanted $250 a night starting for the hotels. I could not believe what my eyes were seeing. So, I said, "I'm not going to pay that amount of money to go and stay at no hotel. They're crazy. What I'm going to do is I'm going to go and stay on International drive in Orlando and I'm going to drive a few minutes and from there I'll stay and go back and forth to the seminars necessary."

When I traveled to the chiropractic seminar, I was driving down Interstate 4 and following the directions that were given on my GPS and it was telling me to get ready to get off on this exit near Walt Disney. As I was getting off of the interstate, I saw what appeared to be a big castle in the distance and I said to myself, "Man, that place is huge!" And as I continued to follow the directions, I found myself making turns and arriving at the entrance of this magnificent structure. I entered into the gate for the convention center parking and I went there and registered for the seminar. I mean, it was a massive number of chiropractors and vendors from all over the United States. And during the break period, I was getting ready to head back to my hotel to pick up and spend some time with my now wife and I remember everybody else going in the opposite direction as myself, as if it was a mass exodus and my spirit said, "Turn around and go and see where they're going." And as I began to walk through the convention hall and crossed over the little catwalk into the main part of the resort, I was almost like a kid in a candy store in such awe at how magnificent this place was looking compared to the smoky, stained room of a severely hot, outdated Holiday Inn. And I'm looking and just like, wow. Just in utter amazement and without words. So, I turned around and I left the resort and I'm driving as fast as I can, to some degree, what seemed like to me and went and got my wife and told her, "Hey, pack up, we're leaving here." She was like, what are you talking about?" I'm like, we're leaving here. We're not staying here another minute."

We left that stinky place and checked ourselves in at the Gaylord Palms for 200 bucks a night. I was in so much awe that the price didn't matter. But, I said to myself then, "Wherever the convention was held, that's where I'm going to stay and I don't care what it costs." If you work hard day in and day out to make your vision become a reality, you need to play and taste the finer things in life because that's a testament to your work. So, don't worry about the money. At the end of the day, it is an expense.

Uncle Sam wants his, so you better get and enjoy yours as much as you can. Experience the fullness of life. Don't hold back from yourself and give so much of you to others. Experience it. Don't cheat yourself. You didn't cheat yourself when you were sacrificing. You didn't cheat yourself when you were in the office or in your shop, your business working late hours. You didn't cheat yourself when you decided to give a discount to this person, that person or the other. You didn't cheat yourself when somebody skipped out and didn't pay the bill.

> **"Enjoy the fullness of life. Don't hold back from yourself and give so much of you to others."**
>
> Dr. Zeboye A. Doctor

You kept pushing!

So, get your R & R because you have been working very, very hard for it. When I went to that seminar, my first seminar as a first year Chiropractor, it motivated me to push and work harder and rejuvenated me to get back in my office to make myself better. It gave me a fire and a passion that I didn't have because I saw what was out there that I did not know anything about. It was a totally different reality from my upbringing and from what my previous experience has shown.

Take those trips. Go on those spiritual retreats. Go to those continuing education seminars. You may have to go and do a little work and everybody else may get a chance to play that's in your immediate circle or family that you have to go and maybe bring with you. But, after the seminar is over, you'll have your time to get a little bit of rest and relaxation and get some thoughts to yourself and think about what you want to do and reflect on what you need to do to make your business stronger so that your company can grow. And that's what those seminars do. You can get around some individuals with like minds that are in the same profession as yourself and gather some ideas from them. That's what R & R does. Fishing does it at times for me. Getting on the road sometimes and just taking a long trip or ride does it for me. And when you can get away to yourself or get around some individuals to just bounce ideas off of, it can help you.

> **"Experience it. Don't cheat yourself. You didn't cheat yourself when you were sacrificing."**
>
> Dr. Zeboye A. Doctor

At the time I was recording this book, I had just left a Gonstead seminar in Atlanta, Georgia and as stated in an earlier chapter, my spirit was just motivated and stirred up and told me to MOVE; told me to LEAVE. And at that point, I couldn't do anything, but move and get out of there because I had gotten what I needed to get from that seminar, which was the push. The "I can't take it anymore!" Not another moment. Not another second. Not another hour. Not another day will go by that I will say that I have not written or started my book.

At this point now, at this stage of the book where you're reading, I'm at that point to where I'm almost finished. And you have a book in you, like someone told me. You have books in you, like someone told me. Get them out. You will feel better. The rest and relaxation is the rejuvenation to go back into your vision and make it better.

When you have a vision, as you do, when you have a business, as you do, and even if it's only in your mind right now, you still have a business because before it becomes a tangible thing that you can see, touch, and feel, you have to hold it in your mind. Do not hold it too long in your mind get it out here so people can see what's in your mind.

Let them see the businesses that you have in your mind.

Let them see really and truly how you think, just how much of a genius you really are.

Show the world just who you are, but most importantly, show yourself.

Chapter 15:

What More Can I Say?

Main Principle

If you work hard, be certain to play hard. The rest and relaxation is the rejuvenation to go back into your vision and make it better.

Throughout the course of this entire book, you have been equipped with the steps that every person should know before they start or while starting a business. You know exactly what needs to be done. So that thing called fear, False Evidence Appearing Real. We've talked about that before. That should be dead and buried. Never ever, ever, ever, ever to rise again. And I would even take that even farther.

Let's dig it up. Let's dig the corpse of fear up, just one more time. Just one more time. And on the corpse of fear, I want you to pour gasoline all over it. I want you to pour a trail about 20 feet away from the corpse of gasoline. And at the end of that trail 20 feet away from that gasoline-soaked corpse, I want you to light the end of that trail and watch the fire go down those 20 or so feet to that corpse soaked in gasoline.

I want you to let that Mother@#$*3r burn because at this point to bury that corpse is a physical change. It's going to take a while for it to totally decay, if it ever will. But, as you learned from your science class and dealing with chemistry, we're going to let that corpse undergo a chemical change.

We're going to change its physical state to where it can never, ever, ever be reversed again You can go and dig up a

---

body. But, if we cremate that corpse, the only thing that is left as the book says are "ashes to ashes and dust to dust."

It's blending in with every other piece of matter that matter came from, the dust. So, you are never ever, ever going to be able to dig up that corpse of fear ever again.

It's gone.

There is no fear.

You never have to speak of fear or worry about fear again because it can never enter into your realm. What more can I say? Need I say anymore?

If you don't think that you have what it takes to start your own business and be successful in business by now, report to work on the next scheduled date. If you don't think that you have enough in you, that you have everything that you need inside of you in order to be and become that which you see in your mind. If you don't know that by now, there is nothing else that I can say, but you are in your OWN way.

Move the hell out of your own way and be the greatness that's in you!!

Thank you for reading this book and giving me the opportunity to put a small part of me inside if you. Spread the word. Thank you and I hope you have enjoyed it.

Appendix A
Start-Up Business Resources

Federal Employee Identification Number (EIN); pertinent forms (W-2, W-4, W-9, 1099, 2553 forms) (www.Irs.gov)

Business name/Legal Structure-
(Division of Corporation for your particular state)

County Sales Tax, Exemptions, etc.-
(Department of Revenue for your particular state)

Copyrighting (www.copyright.gov)

Trademark/Patenting (https://www.uspto.gov)

Business Partnerships/Networking Opportunities (Contact your local Chamber of Commerce)

Business plan (http://bit.ly/samplebusinessplantemplate)

State/Federal Licenses & Permits (if applicable):
- Investment advising (http://www.sec.gov
- Drug manufacturing (http://www.fda.gov)
- Preparation of meat products
  (http://www.fda.gov)
- Broadcasting (http://www.fcc.gov)
- Ground transportation (http://www.dot.gov)
- Selling alcohol, tobacco or firearms
  (http://www.atf.gov)